Under Sail

Written by Jenny Feely
Photography by Michael Curtain

A long time ago, ships did not have motors. These ships were called sailing ships because they had large sails. They used the wind to move them from one place to another.

When the wind blew, the sails helped the ship to move. Sailing ships could sail with the wind, but could not sail directly into the wind.

Sailing ships had a captain and a crew of sailors. The captain was in charge of the ship.

The captain was helped by the first mate and the second mate. They could take over the ship when the captain was resting.

The sails hung from large poles called **yards**. The yards were high up on a **mast**. Sailors put up the sails and took them down.

yards

ratlines

mast

The sailors climbed up narrow rope ladders called **ratlines**. They balanced on ropes while they pulled in the heavy sails or let them out.

Every rope on a sailing ship had a name and a place. The sailors had to learn the name of each rope and where it belonged.

Sailors also had to know how to tie different types of knots. Before a sailor was able to climb the masts or to do other work, he had to learn the ropes.

Sailors had to have good balance. They often worked while the ship was moving up and down in big waves. Waves would wash over the deck and make it slippery.

Sailors had to be careful not to be washed overboard because it was difficult for the ship to sail back to pick them up.

Sailing ships had a carpenter and a sailmaker. The carpenter was able to repair the ship. The sailmaker could mend sails that got ripped in storms.

When the weather was calm, the sailmaker and carpenter would spend their time keeping the sailing ship **"ship shape."**

Carpenter at work

Sailmaker at work

11

Sailors brought their own clothes and bedding when they boarded the ship.

Sailors' beds often were made of **burlap** bags filled with straw. Sometimes, in very rough seas, the sailors' beds would get wet. But the sailors would have to sleep in them anyway.

Sailors ate **salted pork or beef**, and ship's biscuits. Ship's biscuits were very hard. Sailors dipped the biscuits in tea to soften them.

Sailors worked for four hours and then had four hours off. This meant that they could only sleep for four hours at a time.

If a ship was sailing in a storm, the sailors would have to work to keep the ship on course and safe. Then the sailors would have to do without sleep until the storm passed.

Sailing ships would often take more than 100 days to travel to their **destination**. They had to carry enough food and fresh water to last for the whole **voyage**.

Fresh water was used only for drinking and cooking. Salt water was used for cleaning and bathing. Buckets of salt water were kept on deck in case of fire.

burlap	a strong, coarse material
destination	the place where you are going
mast	a tall pole that rises up from the deck of a ship and supports the sails
ratlines	rope ladders used to climb the mast
salted pork or beef	pork or beef that has been covered in salt and dried
ship shape	tidy
voyage	journey
yards	long poles attached to the mast from which the sails hang